TOO COOL
Beach Patrol

Phil Kettle
illustrated by Craig Smith

Black Hills

Distributed in
the United States of America
by Pacific Learning
P.O. Box 2723
Huntington Beach, CA
92647-0723

Website:
www.pacificlearning.com

Published by Black Hills
(an imprint of Toocool Rules
Pty Ltd)
PO Box 2073
Fitzroy MDC VIC 3065
Australia
61+3+9419-9406

First published in the United States by Black Hills in 2004.
American editorial by Pacific Learning in 2004.
Text copyright © Phillip Kettle, 2003.
Illustration copyright © Toocool Rules Pty Limited, 2003.

 a black dog and Springhill book

Printed in China through Colorcraft Ltd, Hong Kong

ISBN 1 920924 15 9
PL-6215

10 9 8 7 6 5 4 3 2 1   08 07 06 05 04

Contents

Marcy

Scott

Dog

Bert

Toocool

Chapter 1
Tower Duty

I loved being in charge of the megaphone.

"Attention all swimmers. Please swim in the safe area."

It was my first day as a lifeguard. I was in the tower by myself.

Well, I wasn't quite by myself. I did have Scott with me. I was the lifeguard, though. If anybody needed saving, it would be Toocool to the rescue.

Scott was still training with the junior lifeguards. He'd probably be there for a few more years.

I'd gotten my junior certification in no time. They said I was their best student ever.

Now I was ready to become the best lifeguard ever.

Toocool - Best Ever

People would visit the beach just to see me. When I wasn't saving people, I'd be signing autographs.

Lifeguard Dog was also on duty. His job was to keep our lunch safe from the seagulls.

4

I looked out from the tower and saw Marcy.

"Swim in the safe area and wear sunscreen," I called.

"Toocool, I would rather drown than let you save me," said Marcy.

"That's fine with me," I said.

"Just remember..." I said.

"Toocool, if you don't shut your mouth, I'll climb up there and squash you like a lemon," said Marcy, before she walked off.

I didn't answer. I had to watch the beach and make sure everybody was safe.

Chapter 2
Beach Patrol

It was time to do some
lifeguard exercises.

I put Bert the Rooster in
charge of tower duty. Scott
and I really needed
to practice.

7

"We'll start with the 'run-swim-run'," I said. This was my favorite training drill. First you ran 100 yards. Then you jumped in the water and swam 200 yards. Then you got out of the water and ran another 100 yards.

"I hate that game," said
Scott. He knew I'd win. I was a
great swimmer and an even
better runner.

"What do you want to do?"
I asked.

"Use our rescue boards,"
said Scott as he grabbed a
board. I grabbed one too.

We raced into the water and paddled out to sea. The waves were fierce as they pushed us back to shore.

We raced to the buoy. I reached it first and beat Scott back to shore.

"Toocool wins!" I cried.

Scott looked mad. You'd think he'd be used to losing to Toocool, the champion, by now.

"How about a game of beach flags?" I asked.

"Okay," said Scott.

We put a beach flag at the bottom of the tower. Then we walked about twenty yards away from the tower.

We lay on our stomachs and waited for the signal.

Dog barked. I was up and running—faster than you could say "great white shark."

I was diving for the flag
before Scott had even moved.

"I missed the signal," he
complained.

Bert the Rooster crowed
from the tower. It was time to
get back to lifeguard duty.

Chapter 3
Lifeguard Lesson

Marcy was back at the tower wearing her swimsuit.

"I'm here to go swimming," she said.

"You know the rules," I said. "Swim in the safe area and wear sunscreen."

Marcy raced into the water.
"Toocool, if you say that
one more time I am going
to squash you like a lemon,"
she said.

It was looking like an easy patrol day. I picked up the binoculars and checked the water. I checked again.

Then I grabbed the megaphone.

"Get out of the water. I repeat, get out of the water. SHARK!"

There were wild screams.
Dog ran around in circles,
barking. Bert the Rooster fell
off the tower. Scott was
standing with his mouth
hanging wide open.

It was up to me to save the
day—Toocool to the rescue!

"Everybody, please remain calm," I ordered through the megaphone. Luckily, everybody raced to the shore. It looked as if the shark would go hungry. Then a single scream rang out.

Chapter 4
Shark!

Through my binoculars, I could see an arm waving. It was Marcy.

Someone needed to be saved. Was it Marcy or was it the shark? I wasn't sure.

I jumped down from the tower and raced to the water.

Scott yelled, "Toocool, don't do it. You could get eaten alive!"

"Toocool, Toocool, you're our hero," shouted the crowd.

I knew I was.

Scott yelled, "Come on, Toocool, it's just Marcy. Don't risk your life."

I was a lifeguard. It was my job to risk my life.

I sprinted into the water and shouted, "Toocool to the rescue! Don't panic, Marcy."

Chapter 5
Rescue

I dove under the first wave. I came up swimming. Luckily, I was an incredible swimmer.

I had almost reached Marcy when I saw the fin circling her. The shark looked ready to attack. I swam faster.

"Toocool! What are you
doing?" asked Marcy.

"I'm saving you from the
shark, Marcy," I said.

"Great idea," said Marcy.
"The shark might eat you and
leave me alone."

It was obvious that she was
in shock.

The shark was a giant—at least thirty feet long. It had changed direction and was heading right for me. Its mouth was wide open.

I moved to one side. The shark just missed me. It turned back and headed for me again. I decided attack was the best form of defense.

I made a fist.

The shark was about to bite. I punched it in the eye. The shark stopped. It looked at me with its good eye. I looked right back. I was too strong for the shark and it knew it. It turned and swam away.

Toocool had faced a terrifying creature from the deep and had won!

I told Marcy I was going to put my arm under her armpit and tow her in.

"Get lost," said Marcy. She was still in shock.

The TV cameras were rolling as I swam to shore.

Chapter 6
Toocool Hero

The crowd went wild as I jogged onto the beach. Cameras clicked.

The crowd was chanting, "Toocool, Toocool, you're our hero, Toocool, Toocool..."

Marcy lay still on the beach. Her eyes were closed. Was she dead?

"You might have to give her mouth-to-mouth resuscitation," said Scott.

"What?" I said.

"You know—the kiss of life," said Scott.

I was a lifeguard. It was my job. Maybe I wouldn't have to go that far, though. I leaned over Marcy. I held her nose.

"Hey! Let go!" she shouted.

The first of many lives saved by the famous Toocool—lifeguard hero.

I was happy I didn't have to give Marcy mouth-to-mouth resuscitation. I know it's my job, but kissing Marcy would be worse than being thrown off a bucking bull.

The End!

Toocool's
Lifeguarding Glossary

Lifeguard tower—A tall structure, with steps that lead to a viewing platform at the top.

Megaphone—A device that makes voices louder than they really are.

Mouth-to-mouth resuscitation— Breathing into someone's mouth when he or she has stopped breathing.

Rip tides—Dangerous underwater currents that can drag you under the water or out to sea.

Toocool's Map
The Patrol Area

Lifeguard Tower

Lemon Tree Island

The Toocool Backyard Beach

Beware of jellyfish and crabs and roosters!

Sea S

Toocool's Quick Summary
Lifeguarding

As early as the 1700s, people in the United States are believed to have saved shipwreck victims in need of help.

Many people believe the first official lifeguarding meeting was held in France in 1878.

In the United States, the first lifeguarding organization was created in 1912.

Lifeguarding clubs have continued to form around the world, and in 1993 the International Life Saving Federation was formed. It meant that lifeguards from all over the world could keep in close touch with each other.

When you're fifteen, you can officially become a lifeguard.

Of course, because I'm so skilled, I didn't have to wait until I was fifteen.

The Shark

Always swim in the safe area — unless you see a shark there.

This species of shark is often confused with a marlin.

Shark Safety-
Usually sharks swim underwater, but in the Toocool Backyard Beach they float to the top! This makes them especially dangerous.

Q & A with Toocool
He Answers His Own Questions

What made you become a lifeguard?

I've always been interested in saving lives. I knew I was a natural when I rescued Bert the Rooster out of Dog's water bowl. Bert was just a young chick at the time.

Why should you swim in the safe, marked area at the beach?

Lifeguards know the best places to swim. We're trained to know these things. Sometimes there are dangerous rip tides, or currents, which can drag a swimmer out to sea. Ropes, flags, or buoys show swimmers the safest place to swim.

Why do lifeguards sit in a tower?

They have to be able to see way out over the water, and they have to be able to see lots of people at once. Sitting up high lets them do that. Sometimes, they sit in really high chairs instead of towers.

What should you do if you find yourself in danger while swimming?

Just raise your hand and stay where you are. This tells the lifeguard that you need help.

Why do lifeguards wear special uniforms?

This makes it easy to spot the lifeguards on the beach, especially if there is an emergency. Also, I look really good in a uniform.

How many people have you saved so far?

I've only actually saved one person so far—Marcy. Oh, and I did save Bert the Rooster.

What kinds of equipment do lifeguards use to rescue people?

They use different kinds of equipment, like rescue boards, which are surfboards made especially to rescue people. Lifeguards also use rescue tubes, which help them tow swimmers to safety.

When can you swim at an unpatrolled beach?

You should never swim at a beach without a lifeguard. If you get into any kind of trouble, there will be no one to help you.

Lifeguarding Quiz
How Much Do You Know about Lifeguarding?

Q1 Where do you learn mouth-to-mouth resuscitation?
A. From Marcy. **B.** From Dog and Bert the Rooster. **C.** From lifeguarding classes.

Q2 What would you do if Marcy were the lifeguard on duty?
A. Go home. **B.** Make sure you didn't swim out too far.
C. Wait till Toocool came on duty before swimming.

Q3 Why do seagulls like being on the beach?

A. To get food scraps. **B.** To watch Toocool. **C.** To check out the surf.

Q4 Should you wear a hat when you are at the beach?

A. Only if you have a really cool hat. **B.** Always. **C.** Only when there are no clouds.

Q5 Should you swim alone?

A. Only if you don't have any friends. **B.** If you're really hot. **C.** No, always swim with a friend.

Q6 Why wear sunscreen?

A. To look good. **B.** To scare Marcy. **C.** To protect your skin from the sun.

Q7 What would you do if you saw a shark?

A. Ignore it. **B.** Get to shore quickly and tell the lifeguard. **C.** Hope it's a vegetarian.

Q8 Why do lifeguards use megaphones?

A. To be annoying. **B.** So that as many people as possible can hear them. **C.** So they can sing opera.

Q9 Who would you rather be saved by?

A. Marcy. **B.** Scott. **C.** Toocool.

Q10 What do you call a run of waves?

A. A set. **B.** A group. **C.** Fun.

ANSWERS

1 C.   **2** C.   **3** A.

4 B.   **5** C.   **6** C.

7 B.   **8** B.   **9** C.

10 A.

If you got ten questions right, you should become a lifeguard. If you got more than five right, you should feel pretty safe at the beach. If you got fewer than five right, stay at home and take a bath.

TOOCOOL

Rodeo Cowboy

Uncle Buck is staying at the Toocool Ranch. **Toocool** and Roberto take a crash course in bull riding. Does **Toocool** have what it takes to be a real cowboy?

Titles in the Toocool series